Meditation Bliss

Meditation Bliss

Inspirational techniques for finding calm

DAVID FONTANA

dbp

DUNCAN BAIRD PUBLISHERS

LONDON

Meditation Bliss
David Fontana

Distributed in the USA and Canada by
Sterling Publishing Co., Inc.
387 Park Avenue South
New York, NY 10016-8810

First published in the UK and USA in 2007 by
Duncan Baird Publishers Ltd
Sixth Floor, Castle House
75-76 Wells Street
London W1T 3QH

Managing Editor: Grace Cheetham
Editor: Ingrid Court-Jones
Managing Designer: Daniel Sturges
Designer: Rebecca Johns
Commissioned color artwork: Lucy Truman
Commissioned line artwork: Asami Mitsuhira for 3+Co.

Library of Congress Cataloging-in-Publication Data Available

10 9 8 7 6 5 4 3 2 1

ISBN-13: 978-1-84483-481-5   ISBN-10: 1-84483-481-6

Typeset in Eurostile and Trade Gothic
Color reproduction by Colourscan, Singapore
Printed in China

For information about custom editions, special sales, premium
and corporate purchases, please contact Sterling Special Sales
Department at 800-805-5489 or specialsales@sterlingpub.com.

Publisher's note:
The information in this book is not intended as a substitute for
professional medical advice and treatment. If you are pregnant
or are suffering from any medical conditions or health problems,
it is recommended that you consult a medical professional
before following any of the advice or practice suggested in this
book. Duncan Baird Publishers, or any other persons who have
been involved in working on this publication, cannot accept
responsibility for any injuries or damage incurred as a result of
following the information, exercises, or therapeutic techniques
contained in this book.

Contents

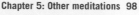

Introduction

Most of us live increasingly busy, hectic and materialistic lives. The stress of living this way can contribute toward a variety of physical ailments, putting our bodies under great strain, and inevitably there is a price to pay. Moreover, this price can be psychological and spiritual, as well as physical.

One way of reducing stress is to change our way of living, but for many people this is neither possible nor necessarily desirable. We need therefore to find other ways, and central to these is to learn how to relax and to make time for personal and spiritual development. Relaxation means not only releasing tensions and relaxing every muscle in the body, it means relaxing the mind, too. And many of us feel a need to find answers to some of the fundamental questions of life and to nurture our spiritual side, which we often neglect. So how can we achieve all this? This book is intended to provide an answer, namely meditation.

In the following chapters you will learn what meditation is, how to do it and the ways in which it can help both mind and body to relax. You will also discover how to recognize what goes on in your mind, as you become aware of mental chatter and learn to replace it with stillness. This ability is the gateway to the profound spiritual realities that transcend the material world and, ultimately, lead to meditation bliss.

From the outside meditation looks easy enough. You only have to sit down and close your eyes. In reality it is not quite that simple. Although you were certainly born with the ability to meditate, lack of use means that you have forgotten, so you need to learn how to use your mind in this way. This book will explore many of the methods involved, such as contemplation (allowing insights about a particular thing to arise) and visualization (conjuring up a mental image upon which to focus). It will also give practical advice about when and where to meditate. As with any undertaking, you will need commitment and patience to succeed, but if you persevere you will find that the benefits of meditation far outweigh the time and the effort you put in.

Relax with meditation

True relaxation means letting go of all tensions in both body and mind, and meditation is one of the best ways to achieve this. In some respects it's more restful than sleep, as even short periods of meditation allow our bodies and minds to renew themselves, to regain emotional and mental balance and to function more effectively and efficiently. Research shows that meditators are calmer, healthier, more alert and better able to concentrate than non-meditators. And contrary to popular belief, meditation doesn't distance you from life – rather, it helps you to live with greater confidence and enjoyment.

What is meditation?

Meditation is a natural process through which we experience our own mind directly. Although there are many different forms of meditation, all have one thing in common, which has been aptly described as "a dwelling upon something" by the psychologists Claudio Naranjo and Robert Ornstein. This means that instead of allowing our mind to become lost in the internal chatter that usually occupies our mental life when we are on our own, in meditation we focus upon a single specific stimulus, such as the breathing, a particular word or set of words, or a special picture or diagram. Gently but persistently our mind returns to this stimulus every time our attention threatens to wander away, simply paying attention to it rather than starting to think about it. No great attempt is made to push thoughts away, since this involves effort. Instead, we take no notice of them. The same is true if emotions arise. We distance ourself from them and our mind remains undistracted.

The natural state of the mind is tranquillity, just as the natural state of the body is relaxation. Once we stop attending to the mental chatter and to the emotional states that usually occupy us, and we relax the physical tensions to which these give rise, our mind returns to its natural tranquil state. This state is what, in essence, the mind actually is, just as water is naturally still unless disturbed. And just as water becomes crystal clear when it is still, so does the mind. As we shall discover as we move through this book, besides relaxing us, the stillness meditation brings allows us to see more clearly into ourselves, and to develop more self-understanding and more self-acceptance.

It is interesting to note that humans are probably not the only species that meditates – it seems that many animals meditate in their own way, too. Watch a cat or a dog lying at ease on the hearthrug. We assume that they are sleeping, but often they may simply be resting with their minds clear and open. This would help to explain their alert attentiveness and their abiding contentment with life.

The history of meditation

Meditation is likely to be as old as humankind itself. From the earliest times, men and women will have sat quietly, their bodies relaxed and their minds free from thoughts. There is no doubt that the ancient Egyptians meditated 5,000 years ago. Some of their earliest wall engravings show kings, queens, priests and gods with their hands resting on their knees and sitting with the typical straight backs of meditators. Similarly, various meditation techniques are mentioned in ancient Indian scriptures which date from around the same time.

However, the earliest systematic account of how to meditate comes from the teachings of Gautama Siddharta – the Buddha – 2,500 years ago. Mindfulness of breathing, which is the method taught by the Buddha, probably goes back even earlier and is still one of the most widely used and effective methods available to us. Focusing on the breath lies at the heart of Eastern spiritual and psychological practices, and is suitable both for beginners and advanced practitioners. As Buddhism spread from India to China, Tibet, Japan and other Asian countries, each developed their own interpretations and meditation techniques.

Meditation also featured largely in the early Christian Church and has always been an important feature of the Russian, Greek and other branches of the Orthodox Christian communities. It is found in Islam, too, through the mystic Sufis, who have used meditation ever since their religion was founded by the Prophet Mohammed in the early seventh century AD. It has taken thousands of years for meditation to become widespread in the West. In the 1960s and '70s many people became fascinated by the cultures of the East, sparking a surge of interest in spiritual traditions and practices, such as yoga and meditation. Now, meditation is inextricably woven into the very fabric of almost every culture and every society known to history. Its very endurance as a practice for body and mind is ample proof of its effectiveness and of the many benefits it brings.

The benefits of meditation

We have already mentioned how meditation can relax the mind and body, reduce stress and lead to greater clarity of mind. These in themselves are major benefits, but there can be many other advantages. Some arise spontaneously, whether you are deliberately looking for them or not, while others depend upon how deeply you go into meditation. For meditation has many different levels, a number of which will be described in this book, together with the various ways in which they have been used by both Eastern and Western cultures.

Among the additional physical benefits of meditation reported are: a reduction in blood pressure; the correction of the tendency to overeat; help with the management of chronic pain; aid with combatting alcohol and drug abuse; and improved posture and body awareness. Among the psychological benefits of meditation cited are: better sleep; improved memory; more control over troublesome emotions such as anger and anxiety; greater tolerance of other people and of minor irritations; increased joy in the simple pleasures of life; and, of course, greater control over thoughts. Many people also claim that after they have been practising meditation for a little while, their families and friends remark that they look healthier and younger, and colleagues comment how they are easier to relate to and work with.

Meditation also brings great benefits to those of us interested in personal and spiritual development – typically, we find greater self-insight; self-understanding and self-acceptance; a greater appreciation of nature; greater compassion toward all living beings; and a sense of gratitude for the gift of life.

At deeper and more profound levels still, meditation can help us to address the fundamental questions about our own existence, such as "Who am I?" and "Why am I here?" It also brings an increasing awareness of the spiritual dimension that underlies all creation and of the unity and love that unites all things. Meditation indeed feeds your mind, body and spirit.

Getting started

Ideally, you should be able to meditate anywhere at any time. Nevertheless, it is helpful to have a designated quiet place in which to practice. Most meditators sit cross-legged on the floor on a cushion that raises them about 4 inches/10cm from the floor. If you find it difficult to sit on the floor, an upright chair is the next best thing. Your clothes should be loose and comfortable. Try to wear similar things every time, so that the act of putting them on turns your mind to meditation, or you can dispense with clothes altogether. When you begin to meditate, aim to sit for five minutes, then gradually extend your practice to 10 minutes. Eventually you may wish to sit for half an hour or more.

Prepare your body

In meditation you need to be able to sit without fidgeting for at least five minutes. As you progress you will learn how to sit still for longer. It is important to have good posture, so always keep your back straight, palms upward and your hands in your lap, one resting lightly on top of the other. Don't let your back and shoulders slump or your head fall forward. As a novice, it's best to close your eyes to minimize distractions, but as you advance you can keep them half open, to stop you from getting too isolated from the outside world.

◆ Sit on a cushion on the floor, cross your legs and slide your bottom forward a little so that you are almost sitting on your left heel. Then, if possible, lift your right foot and place it on the opposite calf (or the other way around if you are left-handed). This position helps your body to remain in balance. However, if you find this position too difficult, just sit with your legs crossed or on a chair with your feet flat on the floor. Close your eyes.

Still your body

It's important to remain still while meditating (unless you are doing a moving meditation – see pp.98–109). Any fidgeting disturbs the mind, which becomes clearer in the presence of stillness. Silence is another very desirable form of stillness, especially for the novice, as noise can be distracting until you become more proficient.

As a beginner you will be sitting for only a few minutes in these early sessions, but meditating for any length of time requires a degree of self-control of both body and mind. In the West, far from being in control of ourselves, most of us are controlled by our bodies and their cravings for creature comforts. But don't worry – your self-control will gradually develop as your meditation practice progresses.

◆ Sit on your cushion on the floor or on a chair. Close your eyes. Check that your clothes are comfortable, then mentally examine your body to make sure it is free from tension. If you detect any tightness, gently contract the muscle and then let it relax. Start with your feet, then work your way up your calf and thigh muscles to your abdomen, torso, hands, arms, shoulders, neck and, finally, your eyes and face. Some slight remaining discomfort is quite natural at first – don't allow it to distract you.

✿ The ability to turn your mind away from minor discomforts is not only mind-strengthening, it provides the basis for pain control, something we all find useful from time to time. By focusing your mind in meditation, you become less conscious of pain, a freedom that you can then extend into daily life.

Watch your thoughts

All meditation practices entail gaining some control over the mental chatter that, when left unchecked, habitually dominates our mental lives. One practice that is good to try is simply watching each thought as it arises, while at the same time remaining independent of it – as if your mind is passively watching clouds passing across the infinite spaciousness of the sky. Make no attempt to judge or to hang on to the thoughts or to react emotionally to them. The emotions are not you, any more than your thoughts are you. They are transitory, impermanent things that arise from emptiness and pass away into emptiness. As a meditator you are simply a dispassionate, objective observer.

Don't worry if at first you find this practice difficult – it is still a valuable exercise for helping you to see how trivial and chaotic the activity of your untrained mind is. Try it for a few minutes to see how your mind works.

Sit on your cushion on the floor or on a chair. Close your eyes and notice how thoughts arise seemingly from nowhere, and how, if you allow it, one thought leads to another, which leads to another, and so on. Watch this train of associations, and note also how thoughts can arouse emotions. Think of a recent incident that provoked strong emotions – for example, a reunion with a long-lost friend that made you feel joyful or a brush with a difficult colleague that set off feelings of indignation and anger. When the emotions – whether pleasant or unpleasant – arise, watch them objectively as you are doing with your thoughts, and notice how, provided you do not lose yourself in them, they quickly go away. If any strong emotions persist, repeat gently to yourself "Let go, let go", and concentrate on staying physically relaxed and mentally objective.

Work with your breath

Deprived of air we quickly die, so it is no exaggeration to say that the breath is the very stuff of life. It is with us always, day and night, and it is a constant reminder of our link with the world around us. The ancients thought that with each breath we draw in the divine spirit. So the act of breathing is one of – if not the – best things upon which to focus in meditation. In fact, watching the breath was the method taught by the Buddha himself 2,500 years ago.

For the meditator deep, steady breathing is the rule. This does not mean taking in huge gulps of air, simply that you draw the breath down to your diaphragm instead of only into the upper part of your lungs.

Always notice and, if necessary, correct your breathing as you meditate. Try to become more aware of it in daily life, too. Notice how slowing your breathing helps to calm and relax you.

◆ Sit on your cushion on the floor or on a chair. Close your eyes, and focus on your normal breathing. Does your breath reach your chest, or does it go right down to your abdomen? Try to draw your breath down through your ribcage to the bottom of your lungs. Feel them expanding. Now, examine the quality of your breathing. Is it rhythmic or irregular, gentle or harsh, slow or fast? Aim to breathe slowly, deeply and rhythmically.

❖ As your practice develops, so your breathing will become softer and gentler. You will also notice a slowing down of your heart-rate and your blood pressure may fall.

Aids to meditation

One of the best aids to meditation is, of course, having a good teacher, a subject to which we return later (see pp. 120–121). Books can also be very helpful. However, a particularly useful aid, especially for beginners, is to sit sometimes in a group with other meditators, so that the group members can support and encourage each other. But try to resist the temptation to watch what other people are doing, and don't rush to share experiences once the session is over. Meditation is not a competition and although sharing ideas on how to overcome problems can be useful, there is always the risk of becoming too influenced by the practice of others instead of working in your own way.

When people meditate together in a group they seem to generate a particular energy. Whether this has to do with the power of shared minds or simply with having the social support of like-minded friends, this energy can greatly encourage you in your practice.

Daily meditations

To make progress in meditation it's important to practise regularly – ideally, every day. Choose any of the daily meditations in this chapter and, as an aid, set an alarm clock to go off after five or 10 minutes to alert you to stop. As you become more experienced, you can extend your session to 15 minutes or dispense with the alarm and finish when you feel ready to do so.

   You also need to decide on the best time of day to meditate – most people prefer mornings, but some favour evenings. And if you have to miss a day here and there, no matter, but try not to miss more than two days in succession.

Be mindful of your breathing

Once you begin to focus on your breathing in meditation, you will notice things about its quality. This may seem strange, as breathing is such a natural activity that we automatically assume we do it correctly. But emotions such as anger, joy and anxiety change the rhythm of our breathing, and typically we breathe rapidly, shallowly and irregularly when we are emotionally-charged, rather than slowly, deeply and rhythmically. By contrast, the breathing of the really advanced practitioner is said to be so soft that it would not disturb a feather placed under the nostrils.

There are two methods of focusing on the breath. In one you place your attention on your nostrils or just inside your nose, while in the other you concentrate on the gentle rise and fall of your abdomen. The first method tends to be preferred by most people, but either is effective and it is largely a matter of personal choice. Try both methods (but not in the same session) to discover which one works best for you.

◆ **Method 1: Sit on your cushion on the floor or on a chair. Close your eyes and focus upon your nostrils or just inside your nose. Concentrate on your awareness of the coolness of the air as you breathe in, and on its warmth as you breathe out. Don't follow the air as it flows into your body. Like a sentry at the gates of a city, stay at your post.**

◆ **Method 2: Sit as in Method 1. Close your eyes and focus on your abdomen. Pay attention to the rhythmical movement of your diaphragm, the muscle that controls breathing. Draw each breath down toward it and don't allow your attention to wander. Let a gentle feeling of gratitude accompany the breath, welcoming it as it enters your body and thanking it as it leaves. Don't try to put this gratitude into words. It is a feeling and not a thought.**

Greet the new day

Life is a wonderful gift. Sadly, we often take it too much for granted, and focus far more on the negative side of things rather than the positive. Gratitude is one of the most important emotions, and expressing gratitude for the gift of life not only helps to lift our spirits, it also confirms that we recognize our blessings. This sense of gratitude can be built into a morning meditation.

One effective way to do this is by visualizing in your mind's eye the spectacular natural phenomenon of a new dawn (see exercise, opposite). Or you could simply focus on gratitude as you breathe in and out. Another good way is to concentrate on the wonder of the act of breathing itself as you breathe in, and on compassion for all beings as you breathe out. Like gratitude, wonder and compassion are two of the most important emotions, and they remind us to live each precious day to the full.

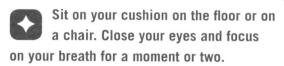 Sit on your cushion on the floor or on a chair. Close your eyes and focus on your breath for a moment or two.

Now, visualize yourself watching a beautiful sunrise. In your mind's eye see the sun slowly appear above the horizon, filling your awareness with the rich, glowing colours of the sky. Reflect on how good it feels to be alive and witness the start of a brand-new day. Give thanks for the sun's warmth and energy, as you bask in its golden rays infusing you with vitality.

After a few minutes, open your eyes. You are now ready to start the day positively, full of enthusiasm for all it may hold.

Recite affirmations

By stilling the conscious mind, meditation opens us to the unconscious – the part of the mind below our conscious awareness that controls most of our bodily functions, influences our thoughts and actions and contains a profound dimension of our real self.

We can use the unconscious to aid personal development through focusing on affirmations during meditation. Affirmations are positive statements about ourselves, such as "I am gaining confidence". They reach the unconscious more easily in meditation and become more effective in producing the desired personal changes. However, it is important not to allow working with affirmations to replace the basic practice of watching your breath.

✦ Sit on your cushion on the floor or on a chair. Close your eyes and focus on your breathing for a couple of minutes to calm your mind. Choose your affirmation and then repeat it with each breath. If the affirmation is short, you can simply say it on the out-breath. If it is longer, divide it between the in- and the out-breath. Repeat for about 5 minutes.

❖ You can use affirmations to improve your physical health, your behaviour, your moods and emotions and for any aspect of personal development. Some people believe that affirmations can bring material rewards, such as wealth, but this is not their true purpose. And you should never use affirmations with the intention of harming others.

Send loving kindness

One of the practices sometimes used in Buddhist meditation as an alternative to focusing on the breath is known as *metta* or loving kindness. Most of us are so bound up in our immediate circle of loved ones that we give little serious thought to anyone else. The *metta* practice will help you to open your heart toward everyone – not just close friends and family, but also to strangers and even to people whom you dislike. The key is to build up your circle of love gradually through practice, venturing further only when you feel comfortable doing so.

Too often we invest time and effort in thinking negtively about people whom we dislike, and our bitterness toward them can last for years and do us as much harm as it may do to them. The *metta* practice helps us to think compassionately and offers a remedy to all this negativity.

Sit on your cushion on the floor or on a chair. Close your eyes and watch your breath. Then, call up thoughts or images of the person or people you love most and direct your deep feelings of love toward them. Next, widen your awareness and summon thoughts or images of your friends and send your warm feelings to them. When you feel ready, widen your awareness further and focus upon acquaintances, and allow your warm feelings to be directed to them. Then, conjure up thoughts about or images of anyone toward whom you feel hostility, and extend your warm feelings to them, too.

As the practice develops we can widen our awareness even further to include all people, animals and plants. Initially, we may find it hard to extend our feelings of loving kindness beyond family and friends, but with practice the circle of our compassion will become wider and more generous.

Receive love

Life and the air we breathe are a gift to us all. None of us "own" these things, we all share them. In meditation, just as we can experience gratitude for the gift of life on each in-breath, so we can experience the love that accompanies the gift of life. One of the features common to mystical experience in all the great spiritual traditions is that ultimate reality is, in fact, love. At some point, in the eternal scheme of things of which we are all a part, each of us will experience this for ourselves.

To open yourself to love while meditating does not require you to use your imagination. Love is already there, otherwise you would not exist. Beyond the tribulations of this world, beyond the world of appearances, is the reality of love, and it is the experience of this love that assures mystics that ultimately all is well.

⬩ Sit on the floor on your cushion or on a chair. Close your eyes and take a moment to acknowledge and reflect that life is given to us as a gift of love, and that our breath represents this. Then, focus on your breathing and how each in-breath symbolizes love. And if you wish, you can accompany the in-breath by softly saying to yourself "I receive love".

Show gratitude

In today's busy world with its emphasis on materialism, it is easy to feel we constantly need *more* of everything. But to find true peace, we need to be able to free ourselves from material trappings. How often do we stop to reflect and give thanks for all the non-material things we already have? While we often tend to dwell on the negative aspects of our lives, through meditation we can learn to appreciate the good things and to count our blessings. Once we start to live in a spirit of gratitude, our lives become even richer and more fulfilled.

⬥ Sit on the floor on your cushion or on a chair. Close your eyes and watch your breath for a few minutes to still your body and mind. Now, call to mind all the good non-material things in your life – for example, the love of your family; the support of your friends and fellow meditators; your good health or the beauty of nature. Return your focus to your breathing and on each out-breath send out gratitude for your blessings. If you wish, you can softly say to yourself, "I give thanks." Use this meditation often to remind yourself that you cannot find true happiness in materialism.

Contemplate an object

People sometimes ask if there is a difference between meditation and contemplation. In a dictionary sense there is very little, but meditators usually take contemplation to differ from meditation in that it is a more active process that involves allowing illuminating insights about the centre of focus to arise. For example, when contemplating a mandala (see pp.64–5) you might ponder its symbolic significance.

Throughout the ages contemplation has been an integral part of spiritual training because it helps to cultivate wisdom and understanding, and encourages empathy and compassion. But it can be used by any meditators in addition to their meditation practice. You can contemplate anything that presents a puzzle, offers a lesson or speaks directly to the higher emotions. Pictures, natural objects, symbols, enigmatic quotations, lines from poetry, and even everyday household items, are just some of the things that lend themselves effectively to contemplation.

◆ Choose your object. Sit on your cushion on the floor or in a chair. with the object at eye level. Focus on your object keeping your mind open, except perhaps to ask "What does this mean?" Do not become lost in any thoughts that arise. Your intention should always be to probe for deeper insights. During the contemplation itself, keep your mind open to receiving spontaneous insights about the object. Once you finish the contemplation, you can go back over any perceptions that arose and work with them at a conscious level.

Learn the inner smile

If you look at a statue or picture of the Buddha, you will see that his face is not only serene, it has the trace of a quiet, gentle smile. You will see a similar smile on the faces of many experienced meditators. What is this smile's significance? It is said that the Buddha smiled because he saw the true nature of all things. In advanced meditators the smile is a sign of deep inner peace. As such, it is a natural result of a certain stage of meditation. The smile also reflects the fact that our fundamental nature is happy. It is only painful life experiences that make us unhappy. The meditator's smile is an inner smile because their whole being is smiling, not just their face.

In meditation, a sense of tranquillity and serenity pervades the whole mind and body and restores inner harmony, and the sense – as Zen Master Dogen taught us – that sitting to meditate is an enlightened act, perfect and complete in itself.

Sit on your cushion on the floor or on a chair. Close your eyes and watch your breathing for a couple of minutes. Now, allow yourself the hint of a smile. Don't make yourself smile – it should not feel forced. Tell yourself that meditating is a happy experience, like seeing a wise and compassionate friend. Smile gently while you focus on your breath for the rest of this session.

Resolve to smile more so that you benefit as much as possible from the health-enhancing substances that the act of smiling releases into the blood stream. Perform the inner smile often and also make an effort to smile more in daily life.

Banish worries

Meditation does not free us from all the anxieties that life brings (unless we are a Buddha or an enlightened being!). Nevertheless, meditators are better able to deal with their anxieties than most people, because they are more adept at distancing themselves from their worries instead of becoming overwhelmed by them.

The act of observing the breath in meditation helps to purify your mind, and the benefits that arise from this become integral to the way in which you look at life. It was the great American writer Mark Twain who said "My life has been full of tragedies and most of them never happened". In fact, most of our worries are unnecessary and many of them are about things that might never happen. And even genuine worries are not helped by worrying about them. If we can do something to lessen our anxieties, we should do it; but if we can't, we should just acknowledge them and put them to one side.

Sit on your cushion on the floor or in a chair. Close your eyes and watch your breath for a couple of minutes. Focus on the transitory nature of each breath. Now, observe any worries that arise in your mind. Just as each breath is transitory, so are many genuine worries. The anxieties do not belong to you, the meditator. Instead of identifying with them, let them gently go and then focus on your breathing once more.

Discover silence

Silence is indeed golden. We sleep best in silence, think best in silence and are usually at our most creative in silence. There is also an affinity between silence and meditation. But the modern world is full of noise – an unrelenting assault on our senses from traffic, loud music, television, and so on.

While advanced practitioners of meditation are able to sit amid noise without distraction, silence is vital for the beginner, if their mind is to become still. However, some people, through habit, find silence disturbing. If this applies to you, don't worry, as it is easy to overcome. Simply retreat into silence as often as you can. If you keep giving your mind the healing experience of silence, it will soon come to appreciate it.

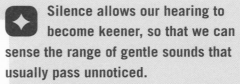

Silence allows our hearing to become keener, so that we can sense the range of gentle sounds that usually pass unnoticed.

In the quietest room in your home, sit on your cushion on the floor or on a chair. Close your eyes and turn your attention to the soft sound of your breathing. Next, focus on the quiet rhythm of the rise and fall of your abdomen. Then, listen to the sound in your ears from the circulation of your blood. These sounds are the music of the body as it returns peacefully to itself.

Go with the flow

Letting go of the past (see pp.94–5) allows us to experience the movement, the flow of all things, including our own lives. Not for nothing has life been likened to a river, which reminds us that, like the river, the flow of time and of our lives is effortless, and that there is a danger in always trying to alter things and arrange the world to suit ourselves. The saying "go with the flow" means accepting what cannot and often what should not be changed, accepting and loving life for what it is and realizing how limited are our powers to fashion it according to our wishes.

✦ Sit on your cushion on the floor or on a chair. Close your eyes and watch your breathing for a moment or two. Notice the rise and fall of your abdomen and feel a sense of impermanence in the moment – in the act of breathing you are going with the flow of life. By going with the flow in meditation, you can come to realize that there is a part of yourself outside time, which is not subject to the change and impermanence of material life.

Be in the moment

The term mindfulness is often used in connection with meditation. It simply means being in the moment and focusing your mind on what you are doing. In meditation this means being mindful of your breathing. In daily life mindfulness is the exact opposite of absent-mindedness – remaining mindful of whatever you are trying to do, whether making your bed, weeding the garden or eating a meal, not only helps you to develop your meditation skills, but also ensures that you perform the task more effectively. If you find your mind wandering at any point when practising mindfulness, just bring it gently back to the present.

In the evening before you go to bed, take a few minutes to mentally run through your day. Sitting somewhere quiet and comfortable, try to recall the day's events in chronological order, or, if you prefer, working backward from the present. If you were paying due attention to what you were doing, you will be able to remember your actions. How well can you remember what happened and what you did? How much detail can you recall? Note the gaps – these reveal the times when you were absent-minded. Resolve to be more mindful tomorrow. Repeat the exercise every night for two weeks to see how much you can improve your mindfulness.

Developing mindfulness not only helps you to perform tasks more efficiently and aids your memory – even more importantly, it helps to give meaning to your life. And as you become more mindful of how you are living, your life events will gain new meaning and you will grow in self-knowledge and self-understanding.

Weekend meditations

Once you can sit for about 15 minutes, you are ready to progress to longer and deeper meditations. Aim to build up each session to about 30 minutes. The weekend is a good time to do this, as you are likely to have more time to devote to your practice.

In this chapter you will find a range of meditations to aid your development and to help you with particular life circumstances. You will learn how to tune in to nature, to explore your senses and to solve problems. There are also meditations to help you to boost your self-esteem and assertiveness, and let go of the past and accept change.

Meditation and nature

Meditation is a natural process and a way of returning the mind to its essential undisturbed state. It is not surprising, then, that meditators usually feel a deep love for the world around them as well as for their own inner world.

Sadly, modern life tends to divorce us from nature. This loss of our natural roots impoverishes us, depriving us of experiencing our shared heritage. Practising meditation outside in the countryside or in a garden is a good way to redress this and to reconnect with nature. Some meditators report that wild creatures seem drawn toward them when they meditate in the open. A well-known meditation teacher in India told me that once, when meditating in a remote spot, she opened her eyes to see an adult tiger crouching in front of her watching her intently. They looked at each other calmly for some minutes until the tiger got to its feet and silently walked away. She and the tiger were simply fellow beings in harmony with each other.

Meditate in natural surroundings, such as a park or a garden, as often as you can. If you have a garden, you can designate a special area for meditation. Zen Buddhism, which lays great emphasis on the natural world, teaches that such a place should be simple, with an atmosphere of harmony and peace. If possible, it should contain both plants and natural materials, such as rocks and stones, and even water. Above all, choose a place in which you can feel a sense of unity with all creation while you meditate.

Consider the elements

Since the earliest times humankind has encountered the natural world through the elements of earth, water, air and fire. Today, we still experience nature in this way, whether we are enjoying the feeling of the sun on our body or the wind in our hair. Indeed, such feelings help us to feel truly alive.

However, as well as connecting to the elements outwardly through the weather, we can also experience them internally, because our bodies are made up of these elements (see exercise, opposite). In this way, nature lives and breathes within us as well as all around us.

◆ Sit on your cushion on the floor or on a chair. Focus your awareness on your body – feel its connection with the earth as your weight sinks into the cushion and your feet rest on the floor. Now, focus on the liquid nature of your body – around seventy percent of it consists of water – and concentrate on the blood circulating through your veins and arteries. Next, turn your attention to the fire of life within you. Feel the heat your body generates to keep you warm. Then, become aware of the air that you are drawing down into your lungs to circulate the oxygen in your blood. Reflect on how life would be impossible without the elements, and give thanks for them.

Contemplate a flower

There are many wonderful creations in nature and one of the most beautiful is surely the flower. Who can fail to be moved by the sight of a field of daffodils, a carpet of bluebells or a single, perfect rosebud? But even if you are lucky enough to live in an environment rich in flowers, chances are that you tend to take them for granted and rarely look at them in detail.

Using a flower as a focus for contemplation, can not only help you to appreciate its intrinsic beauty, but it can also lead you to consider its place in nature and the cycle of life, death and rebirth, which we experience through the seasons. All life is impermanent, and by coming to terms with the transience of our own lives, we free ourselves to live in the present and to become more loving and compassionate beings.

✦ Choose a flower in your garden or the countryside and sit near it (but don't pick it!). Or buy a flower from a florist or a market. Focus on the flower. Now, gently touch its petals and leaves, noting their texture, their fragility. Smell the flower's scent and breathe it in. Looking at the flower, think about how it grew from a tiny seed into a beautiful bloom. But how will it look next week, next month? Consider how it will fade, produce its own seeds and eventually wither, die and return to the earth. Like the life of a flower, our lives, too, are impermanent. Taking inspiration from the flower, resolve to live your life purposefully and mindfully.

Discover your subtle energy

According to yoga, tai chi and other similar Eastern practices, the air carries a subtle form of energy in addition to oxygen and other gases. Known as *chi* in China and as *prana* in India, this energy circulates in the body and represents our life force. The Chinese practice of acupuncture is based upon similar teachings, as is the Indian theory that the body has seven energy centres or *chakras* (see opposite) that help to concentrate and distribute our subtle energy. Although science has not yet verified the existence of this energy, it has discovered that the channels or meridians used in acupuncture, along which the energy is said to flow, show a variation in electrical conductivity from the rest of the body.

Eastern traditions also teach that we can use our breathing to direct subtle energy to re-energize or to heal our body (see exercise, opposite). You can incorporate this technique into your meditation sessions whenever you wish.

Sit on your cushion on the floor or on a chair. Close your eyes and watch your breathing for a moment. Then, as you breathe in, visualize white light entering your body at your lowest chakra (see figure, right) and rising up to your heart chakra in the chest. As you breathe out see the white light rise further still to your crown chakra at the top of your head. After doing this exercise, many people report finding their whole body full of a new lightness and vitality, as if invigorated and purified. Alternately, to help to heal a particular area of your body, visualize drawing white light in on your in-breath, and then imagine directing it to the area you wish to heal on your out-breath.

Gaze at a mandala

Although it is better to keep your eyes closed when you first meditate, for some techniques you do need to open them. For example, in Soto Zen (one of the two main schools of Zen Buddhism), the meditator focuses upon a blank wall and returns the attention to this every time it wanders away. Another popular visual technique is to use a mandala – a symbolic image or "map" of consciousness and cosmic forces.

In Tibetan Buddhism the mandala is traditionally constructed as a symbolic plan of a palace with gates at the four cardinal points, and most Eastern mandalas follow similar ideas. These mandalas contain an arrangement of geometrical shapes and some also feature figures of Buddhas and deities. Mandalas that do not include figures are known as *yantras*.

However, in the West, any profound symbol, such as a circle or a square, can be used. Thanks to their symbolic power, all mandalas and yantras act as a key to deeper levels of the mind and are a valuable addition to meditation practice.

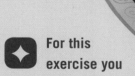 For this exercise you will need a mandala. You can use the one on this page, choose a mandala from a book on the subject, or even design your own. If you wish to make your own, use a geometric shape such as a circle or a square as your starting point, then add the symbols that have a particular resonance for you.

Place your mandala at eye-level, then sit on your cushion on the floor or on a chair. Now focus on the mandala. Don't consciously try to attach meaning to it, allow its symbolism to do the work for you. If, after a while, you can visualize the mandala clearly in your mind's eye, you can close your eyes as you continue to meditate.

Recite a mantra

Sound can be a distraction in meditation, which is why background music is not recommended. However, the sounds of mantras are an exception. Mantras consist of a word, a phrase or a sound, which you say or chant repeatedly as a focal point in place of the breathing during meditation. (In Christianity, Roman Catholics use "Hail Mary, Mother of God", while in the Eastern Orthodox Church "Lord Jesus Christ have mercy on me" is popular.) Certain words, such as "Peace," or "Blessings" can also be used, as they have an important quality of sound. Alternatively, you can use a positive affirmation (see exercise, opposite and pp.34–5). Whatever mantra you use, make sure that you are not distracted by pondering its meaning – try to allow the words to speak for themselves.

A mantra can also be used outside meditation. Simply hold it in your mind throughout the day and repeat it silently when you wish to quieten your thoughts.

Sit on your cushion on the floor or on a chair. Choose the mantra you wish to use and then recite it silently or out loud, synchronizing it with your in- or out-breath or both. As with your breathing, let your mind hold on to the mantra and return to it each time your attention wanders away. If you wish, you can instead use a positive affirmation, such as "I am happy and peaceful" or "I am growing in love". Repeat the mantra for about 5 minutes.

Chant *OM*

Many of the great spiritual traditions teach that the universe came into existence in response to a sound uttered by the Creator, so certain sounds are said to possess the creative force. In the Hindu and Buddhist traditions, mantras (see pp.66–7) usually represent the names of God or of a special teacher or guru, and typically these consist of Sanskrit or Tibetan words. For example, the words "*Om Mani Padme Hung*" (usually translated as "Hail to the Jewel in the Lotus" or "Hail to the Light Within") are said to carry special power in their sounds.

When you are beginning to meditate, it is a good idea to use a simple mantra, such as the Sanskrit sound "*OM*," which is probably the most well-known mantra of all. Interestingly, many people have reported that chanting "*OM*," has a discernible physical effect on their body as well as on their mind and spirit. Some meditators break this mantra into three parts, which are pronounced "A-U-M" (see opposite).

Sit on your cushion on the floor or on a chair. Think of the Sanskrit sound "*OM*", which is pronounced "A-U-M" (phonetically R-OO-MM). Start by taking a deep breath and sounding the "A" in the back of your throat – feel it resonate in your solar plexus. Next, move on to the "U", which you sound in the roof of your mouth but feel in your chest. Then, sound out the "M", which vibrates your lips and reverberates in your head. Repeat the sounds about 12 times, noting the effect that the mantra has on your body and mind. After this meditation people frequently report feeling re-energized, often experiencing a tingling sensation in the body and a new sense of clarity in the mind.

Contemplate music

It is no surprise that throughout the centuries humankind has associated music with the gods. There is no doubt that good music is deeply mystical and it has been used since the earliest times to alter the consciousness of worshippers toward spiritual realities. In theory, then, it should also be an ideal subject for meditation, whether as a main focus or to have in the background. The problem is that the sheer complexity of music takes us to so many levels of experience that we find it difficult to hold our minds still while it is playing.

But while music is not recommended for meditation, it can certainly be used for contemplation. This process (see exercise, opposite) is very relaxing. While contemplating music you may also experience profound spiritual insights and find that striking visual images pop in to your mind, bringing a deep state of inner peace to your body, mind and spirit.

Choose your music – something gentle and uplifting is usually effective – and set it to play. Sit somewhere comfortable and relaxing, such as on a sofa or in an armchair. Close your eyes and relax your body. Listen to the music, absorbing yourself totally in its rhythms, cadences and tones, allowing it to take your mind where it will. When the music has ended, notice how you feel. Calmer? More positive? Inspired, even? The changes in your mood induced by contemplating music can help to transform the way you see the world and how you think about and experience your own existence.

Meditate with scent

Our sense of smell is typically the least used of our senses, yet scents have a particular power to alter our moods and to evoke memories. They can also be a valuable aid to meditation, a fact recognized over the centuries by all the great spiritual traditions – for example, Christians, especially Roman Catholics, use incense in their services, while Hindus and Buddhists light it in their temples.

One explanation for the power of incense is that it is distilled from plants traditionally held sacred. Another is that the great traditions recognize that spiritual practices, such as rituals and meditation, are more effective if they appeal to all the senses: chants and mantras to hearing; mandalas to sight; breathing awareness to touch; wine and sacraments to taste; and, of course, incense to smell. In addition, the scent of incense is thought to purify the air and the surroundings, and to ascend to heaven as an offering to the Divine.

Select incense that produces little smoke and has an appealing scent – traditional favourites for meditation include sandalwood and frankincense. Light your incense mindfully at the start of your meditation session and place it in an incense holder on a metal tray to ensure its safety. Then, focus on your breath for a moment or two. The scent will pervade and linger not only in the room but also on your clothes and skin.

This "odour of sanctity" will help to calm your mind and, over time, you will come to associate it with the meditative state.

Focus on taste

Like the sense of smell, we also make less use than we should of our sense of taste. The high sugar and salt content of many convenience foods tend to blunt our palates, and the frantic pace of modern life means that eating becomes a matter of refuelling our bodies, rather than an experience of taste and real enjoyment.

One way to appreciate your food more is to be mindful when you eat. Usually, even if we are not talking, we are watching TV or doing something else while eating, so it can be revealing to eat a meal or a snack in silence and without distractions.

Mindfulness of eating is a meditation in itself. On retreats and in monasteries meals are taken in silence, to enable those eating to concentrate fully on the food and its taste. You take each mouthful with gratitude as a gift, and savour each morsel to the full while holding your mind still. In this way the different textures and flavours of the food can be fully registered by your senses.

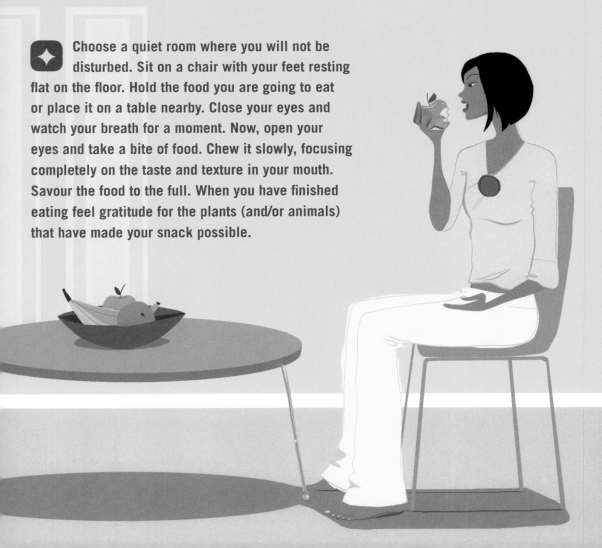

Choose a quiet room where you will not be disturbed. Sit on a chair with your feet resting flat on the floor. Hold the food you are going to eat or place it on a table nearby. Close your eyes and watch your breath for a moment. Now, open your eyes and take a bite of food. Chew it slowly, focusing completely on the taste and texture in your mouth. Savour the food to the full. When you have finished eating feel gratitude for the plants (and/or animals) that have made your snack possible.

Visualize a rainbow

Just as we depend upon the air we breathe and the food we eat for life, so we also depend upon the gift of light, which is a recurring theme in all the spiritual traditions. Meditators speak of "enlightenment" and of the "clear light of bliss", which in Buddhism signifies ultimate reality. Light is composed of the colours seen in the rainbow or refracted through a prism. Not surprisingly, then, the rainbow is seen as a symbol of revelation, of the bridge between heaven and earth.

Rainbows are also said to purify space, and to have healing and tranquillizing properties. The four principal colours of the rainbow – red, yellow, green and blue – are thought to represent respectively fire, air, earth and water, and thus to bring the meditator into closer contact with the elements that make up physical reality. The colours of the rainbow also correspond to the seven chakras (see pp.78–9).

◆ Due to their fleeting nature, it is difficult to use rainbows that form in the sky as a focus for meditation. A good substitute is to place a crystal in a window where it throws rainbows onto the walls, or you can use a picture or a photograph. Sit on your cushion on the floor or on a chair. Focus on the rainbow and meditate upon its symbolic properties and the blessings that light so freely bestows upon us.

Light up your chakras

As we have seen (see pp.62–3), the chakras – our centres of subtle energy – are widely recognized by practitioners of complementary medicine. Each of the seven chakras is associated with a colour (or colours): the base chakra (in the perineum) with red; the sacral chakra (just below the navel) with orange; the solar plexus chakra with yellow; the heart chakra (in the chest) with green and pink; the throat chakra with blue; the third eye chakra (between the eyebrows) with indigo; and the crown chakra (at the top of the head) with white or violet.

Working with the colours of the chakras can help to redress the imbalances that occur when there are blockages or disturbances in our flow of subtle energy. In the meditation opposite you can focus on the colours of the chakras by visualizing drawing in your breath at the base chakra and watching it "light up" each chakra in the associated colour as it travels up to the crown chakra.

⬥ Sit on your cushion on the floor or on a chair. Close your eyes and on the first in-breath visualize white light entering at the base chakra, which glows a brighter red in response. Picture your second breath entering in the same way but flowing up to the sacral chakra, which shines orange. Then, on your next breath, imagine the light reaching the solar plexus chakra, which glows yellow. In subsequent breaths imagine the light reaching in turn the heart chakra (green or pink), the throat chakra (blue), the third eye chakra (indigo) and finally the crown chakra (white or violet).

In your mind's eye, envision each chakra radiating light in its own colour and, finally, imagine all of them glowing at once. Rebalancing your chakras in this way will boost your sense of well-being.

Explore your dreams

Progress in meditation can have a profound effect upon your dream life, because the powers of attention you learn in meditation continue during dreaming and make your dream experiences more vivid and memorable. Also, meditation opens you to your unconscious and to the deeper levels from which your dreams arise.

Dreams from the personal unconscious relate to events in daily life and to anxieties, hopes and fears, while those that arise from the collective unconscious (the part of the mind linked to our inborn, spiritual nature) are more profound and have a deeply symbolic content. As a result, meditation is very useful for working with dreams, particularly as a path toward spiritual illumination.

✦ If you wish to explore your dreams, keep a notebook by your bedside and jot down your dreams on awakening. This dream diary will not only tell your unconscious that you wish to take dreams seriously and recall them each morning, but will also help you to identify the recurring themes in your dream life, which provide the most revealing information. Many of these themes are symbolic. The meaning of some symbols, such as a key, a suitcase or a wise person may be obvious, while others such as water, a house or an animal may be less so.

When you identify a particularly strong or recurrent symbol, try to discover its meaning by writing down all the words you associate with it in a circle around the symbol. Then, see which word connects most closely with it. Ask your unconscious to guide you.

Balance yin and yang

We are all made up of opposite (or yin and yang) elements – that's what makes each of us so interesting. Meditation helps us to make these elements work in harmony with each other, balancing mind and body as well as mind and spirit. When you meditate in the classic position, even your posture represents a balance, with your crossed legs, bottom and erect spine forming a symmetrical triangle.

A good visual symbol of this balance is the yin–yang diagram (see opposite), which depicts two shapes, light and dark, enfolding each other. These opposites complement each other rather than cancel each other out – either can be in the uppermost position in the yin–yang diagram, just as our personality leans toward one or other element. Whether male or female, introvert or extrovert, we can all stay true to our unique selves by finding and maintaining a happy equilibrium.

✦ Sit on your cushion on the floor or on a chair. Close your eyes and watch your breath for a moment. Now, take a moment to think about your yin and yang qualities – for example, your introverted, inward-looking side and your extroverted, outgoing side, or your assertive side and your yielding side. Visualize two of these elements as part of the yin–yang symbol (you can open your eyes and focus on the diagram on this page if you find this easier). Notice how one part would be meaningless without the other. Each element encloses some of its opposite, so that they can meld together to create a harmonious balance.

✤ We all need a balance of ying and yang. When the mind rediscovers its natural state during meditation, these opposites achieve the state of harmony that helps the development of a mature and happy personality.

Ponder a koan

Most of us enjoy puzzles, but if we were asked to "show me your face before you were born", we might dismiss the question as paradoxical, because once we are in this world there is no way in which we can show the face we had before we came into it. Yet such paradoxical questions, known as *koan*s, are practical tools used in Zen meditation to refine the meditator's mind.

The two main approaches to resolving koans are to hold the koan in your mind until the meaning comes to you in a flash of insight or to contemplate it analytically to probe its meaning directly. Ideally, you should be given a koan by a Zen master, who selects it for you personally, but you can still choose a koan yourself, providing you don't assume that your insights are correct and that you have resolved it – only a Zen master who has resolved it him- or herself can judge this. Practising with koans can help you to still your mind and to observe what arises in the stillness.

✦ Sit on your cushion on the floor or on a chair. Close your eyes and watch your breath for a moment. Now bring to mind the koan, "What is the sound of one hand clapping?" Hold it in your mind. If you wish, you can imagine that you are asking the question to a wise friend who listens but does not reply.

There is no one, right answer, there are only insights. If, initially, nothing comes to mind, don't worry – simply persevere.

✿ How can paradoxical questions refine the mind? Firstly, they help us to develop intense motivation. Knowing that the koan *can* be resolved often awakens in us a fierce desire to do so. Secondly, koans emphasize the paradoxical nature of life itself, yet remind us that the koan of life can also be resolved. And thirdly, paradoxical questions help us to develop our powers of concentration as we impel our mind to keep working upon them as often as we can.

Solve a problem

As with a koan (see pp.84–5), one of the best ways to solve a problem is by holding it in your mind without making a conscious attempt to solve it, allowing insights to arise. This hands the problem over to the unconscious, rather in the way that you sleep on a problem, except that by contemplating it you take it even deeper into the unconscious and emphasize the need to solve it. As with all meditation, it's important to remain unhurried – the unconscious must be allowed to take its own time to find a solution.

Another approach is to analyze the problem during contemplation (see pp.42–3). Both ways can be equally effective, and much depends upon the nature of the problem and personal preference.

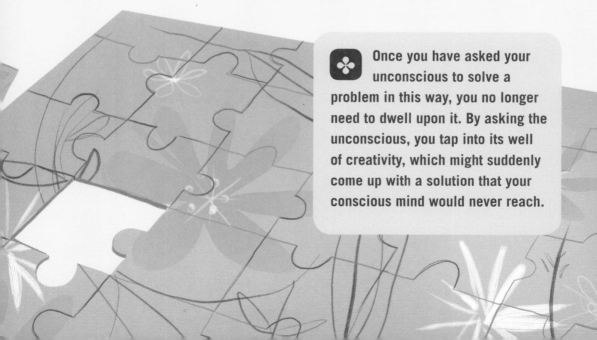

★ Think of a problem and hold it in your mind without conscious deliberation but with confidence that you will find an answer. Phrase the problem in short, clear language so that your unconscious mind can readily understand it (for example, "What shall I do about … ?" or "What is the answer to … ?"). When insights arrive in your conscious mind, don't treat them as inevitably correct. Your unconscious is proposing possible solutions rather than definitive conclusions. Now, your conscious mind needs to consider them objectively and decide on their accuracy and suitability. If the solutions are not acceptable, return once again to the problem and wait for fresh insights.

❖ Once you have asked your unconscious to solve a problem in this way, you no longer need to dwell upon it. By asking the unconscious, you tap into its well of creativity, which might suddenly come up with a solution that your conscious mind would never reach.

Improve listening skills

The world is full of talkers but there are far fewer good listeners. Even when we are supposed to be listening, our attention is often either on our own thoughts or watching what is going on around us. The ability to filter out sounds can be valuable, but not when it leads to absent-mindedness – our minds being literally "absent" from the present moment.

Meditation develops our listening skills because it teaches us to pay attention, so that even when we're not meditating, we can decide where to place our attention, and keep it there with little effort. When someone is talking we can focus completely upon what is being said.

Sit somewhere quiet and comfortable, preferably outdoors or by a window. Watch your breathing for a couple of minutes. Now, listen to the sounds you hear around you: the wind, bird song, the rustle of the trees, or if you are in an urban setting, the hum of traffic. Pick a particular sound and give it your full attention. Focus on this sound for as long as you can.

The ability to pay attention brings many benefits. It improves your memory, allowing you to recall what has been said and heard, fostering interest and a greater engagement with life. When faced with unwanted sounds, you can focus elsewhere instead of being distracted or angered by them. You are able to direct your mind at will.

Believe in yourself

Self-belief has nothing to do with excessive pride or with an inflated sense of our own importance, it is simply a realistic assessment of our own abilities, whether already realized or potential. If we know our own abilities, we know what we can do, and we have confidence in our capacity to achieve it.

Self-belief represents a necessary level of self-acceptance. We aim to improve ourselves, but we also accept where we are at present, and recognize that we should be grateful for who and what we are. Put another way, self-belief means that we are at home in ourselves.

Sit on your cushion on the floor or on a chair. Watch your breath for a couple of minutes. Then, think of yourself with compassion and recite an affirmation, such as "I believe in myself", or "I accept myself as I am", with every out-breath. You can reinforce the positive effect of the affirmation outside of meditation by repeating it 5 times every morning on waking and 5 times before you go to bed at night, and at any other time, as necessary.

Through using affirmations we can remind both the conscious and unconscious to make use of our full potential. With our growing ability to pay proper attention to what we are doing, we become increasingly effective at what we do. And at a deeper level, meditation helps us to be more our own person. We spend many of our formative years being told that we should be somebody we are not. Meditation returns us to ourselves and helps us to remember who we really are.

Learn to say "no"

Often it is much easier to say "yes" than to say "no". As a result, we sometimes find ourselves taking on too many commitments or agreeing with opinions and ideas with which we really disagree. We dislike the idea of disappointing others, and their powers of persuasion are often difficult to resist.

However, the development of self-belief that meditation can bring provides you with the confidence to know your limits as well as your strengths. A sense of your own limits allows you to recognize that no one is indispensable and that other people are often better equipped to help than you are.

Self-assertion does not mean arrogance, selfishness or imposing your will on others. Meditation also teaches humility and compassion. It means that you believe in yourself and, freed from unecessary self-doubts, you have the courage to defend the truth, the rights and the freedom of all beings.

Meditation improves your concentration levels and hence your ability to listen closely and to make better judgements. This, in turn, helps you to prioritize tasks and requests for your help. If you are clear and fair-minded in your decisions, people will generally like and respect you for it.

Sit on your cushion on the floor or on a chair. Watch your breath for a moment. Call to mind a recent situation in which you wish you had been more assertive. Replay the incident in your mind's eye, but this time imagine yourself graciously saying "no". Notice how you feel when you do what you believe to be right. Then, visualize the person whom you have disappointed reacting in an understanding and accepting manner. Feel empowered and resolve to be more assertive in future.

Let go of the past

Time is a mystery. We live in a universe bounded by space and time, yet we know little about the real nature of time. In fact, "time" is really only a concept that we have invented to explain the constant process of change in our world – a process that means the second through which we have just lived is as irrecoverable as the first second of time. Yet we all tend to cling to the past and think longingly of things that are gone, such as our childhood or our former relationships.

The realization that the past is irrecoverable often brings sadness. Meditation can help you to release this sadness by encouraging you to replace it with gratitude. Think about all the wonderful moments you have been priveleged to experience in your life and give thanks that you have been lucky enough to have had them. Then, bring your focus gently back to the present and express your gratitude for the present moment and the gift of life.

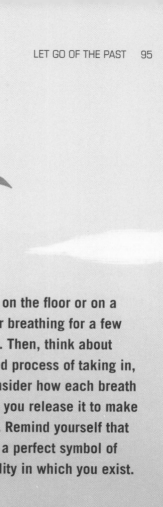

Sit on your cushion on the floor or on a chair. Focus on your breathing for a few moments to still your mind. Then, think about how breathing is a repeated process of taking in, holding and letting go. Consider how each breath lasts for its own time, then you release it to make space for your next breath. Remind yourself that breath is life and it is also a perfect symbol of the eternal space-time reality in which you exist.

Accept change

There's nothing we can do to stop things changing – even if we often feel that we might like to. All created things, including the planet beneath our feet, are constantly shifting and evolving. What we call "time" is, in fact, this very process of change, which we measure by the position of the Earth in relation to the Sun and then divide into minutes, hours, weeks and so on.

As change is inevitable, accepting it can save us from disappointment. After all, change isn't necessarily bad. Think of the rhythm of the seasons, the ebb and flow of the tides, the light of dawn, the opening of a flower and the cool of evening. Remember the excitement of children as they welcome their birthdays, or the joyful celebrations we hold to mark a wedding. When you learn to accept change, you find it easier to go with the flow and your approach to life becomes more relaxed.

◆ Sit on your cushion on the floor or on a chair. Close your eyes and imagine a world without change – a dead place, static and motionless. Now, contrast this image with a world pulsing with life, constantly evolving and progressing, a vibrant place in which everything has its own time and space. Consider how you are part of the ever-changing yet unending nature of life through the continual coming and going of your breath. Realize that, just as a chrysalis becomes a butterfly, things change only their form and not their essence. Beyond such changes of form is the eternity from which all things come.

Other meditations

Usually when we speak of meditation, we are thinking of sitting meditation. However, by remaining mindful while carrying out certain tasks, we are, in a sense meditating at other times, although it can be difficult to retain the degree of focus we have when sitting. There are also specific forms of moving meditation – good examples include the Zen Buddhist practice known as *kin-hin* and aspects of yoga and chi gong. And by becoming totally absorbed in activities such as painting and writing we can turn these creative pursuits into meditations, too.

Practise *kin-hin*

The Zen Buddhist practice known as *kin-hin* is a type of walking meditation. Essentially, it involves putting your whole attention on the movement of your body rather than simply on your breathing.

As *kin-hin* is best done in a straight line, it is a good idea to perform it either in a long room or outside. Practise initially on a hard, flat surface, but as you make progress, you can also try it on an uneven surface, such as rough ground outside. *Kin-hin* is wonderful for deepening your powers of concentration and enhancing relaxation and balance during movement.

1 Stand upright but relaxed. Make a fist of your left hand and place it horizontally against your abdomen just above the navel. Now, hold your left fist lightly with your right hand (or, reverse the hands if you prefer).

2 Focus your attention fully upon the movement of your right foot as you very slowly lift it off the ground and then place it down again in a short step forward. Synchronize your breathing with your walking.

3 Repeat with your left foot, then your right, and so on. After about 12 steps, turn round mindfully and walk back to your start point. Continue walking back and forth in this way for about 48 steps, or longer if you wish.

Sense a ball of energy

Another good way to explore meditation in movement is through chi gong, an ancient practice, which was first developed in China in the 7th century BC, designed to make the subtle energy or chi (see pp.62–3 and 78–9) circulate more effectively around the body.

The carefully constructed movements of chi gong act like internal acupuncture, synchronizing with your breathing and focusing your mind upon what your body is doing. Many practitioners use chi gong as an integral part of their daily meditation.

1 Stand with your feet parallel and shoulder-width apart, arms hanging loosely by your sides. Bend your knees slightly, draw up your abdominal muscles and tuck your tailbone under.

2 Raise your hands so that they are in front of your lower abdomen with your palms facing each other. Imagine you are holding a ball of energy between your hands.

3 Slowly move your hands shoulder-width apart and see if you can sense the ball of energy expanding between your palms. Then, move your hands closer together again and "feel" the ball contracting. Expand and contract the ball of energy several times, noticing any sensations in your hands.

Touch the sea, look at the sky

This chi gong meditation is both energizing and refreshing. When you perform the meditation for the first few times, focus mindfully on the movements. Then, try it with a visualization. For the first movement, imagine you are standing in the ocean – you touch the water as you put your hands on your knee. Similarly, when doing the third movement, visualize looking at the blue sky above, flecked with white clouds.

1 Place your left foot in front of your right foot, and bend forward, keeping your spine straight. Put your hands one on top of the other on your left knee.

2 Gradually transfer your weight onto your right leg, as you bring your spine upright. Lift your arms out in front of you, keeping your elbows slightly bent.

3 Shift your weight back as far as you can. Raise your arms slightly above the level of your head and push your elbows out to the side. Return to the starting position and repeat the exercise with your right foot forward.

Yoga: Mountain pose

Yoga is another practice closely linked to meditation. Hatha yoga, the type most widely practised in the West, consists of a range of bodily poses, known as *asanas*, which are designed to channel subtle energy through the chakras (see pp.62–3 and 78–9) to the head, calming the mind and bringing spiritual illumination.

Mountain pose is a good posture for beginners to learn, as it forms the starting position for all the standing *asanas*, but it is also a posture in its own right. Although it is a moving meditation, mountain pose particularly promotes stillness. Straightforward to perform, it is associated with the stability and strength of mountains and it helps you to develop good posture and mental clarity.

1 Stand with your feet parallel and hip-width apart. Relax your shoulders, raise your chest upward and outward, and tuck in your chin slightly to lengthen your neck.

2 Breathe in and move your arms forward, then up over your head while pushing up onto tiptoes. Breathe out and lower your arms. Repeat six times.

Yoga: Tree pose

This yoga pose helps you to develop balance and groundedness, while stilling and calming the mind. In much the same way as your emotions and thoughts can strongly affect your body, so improving your physical balance can promote mental equilibrium.

To help you balance you can visualize yourself as a tall, strong tree firmly rooted in the earth. Or imagine that there is a line running down the centre of your body. Try to feel the stillness at this point of perfect balance between the left and right energies of your body.

1 Stand with your feet parallel and hip-width apart. Relax your shoulders, raise your chest upward and outward, and tuck in your chin slightly to lengthen your neck.

2 Shift your weight onto your fight foot, and bring your left knee up toward your chest, clasping it with both hands.

3 Place the sole of your left foot on the inside of your right thigh at a 90-degree angle. Keep both hips square. Bring your hands together in front of your chest and focus on a static object to help you balance. Repeat, standing on your left foot.

Meditation and creativity

We have seen how meditation allows us to become more open to our unconscious (see pp.34–5). A benefit of this is that as our meditation practice progresses, our creativity improves. Creative ideas arise from the unconscious, often spontaneously, and it seems that once the conscious mind recognizes an idea, the unconscious incubates it before suggesting ways to put it into practice.

While creativity is obviously essential in the arts, it is equally important in the sciences. Some scientists, including Einstein, have been profoundly mystical thinkers, accepting even that the source of their own genius remains a mystery. Others say they obtained their best ideas in dreams or when their minds were still and quiet.

Of course, creativity can never be forced, and to a large degree it depends upon inspiration. By stilling your mind in meditation you can tap into the source of inspiration and open up to the quiet voice of your own particular genius.

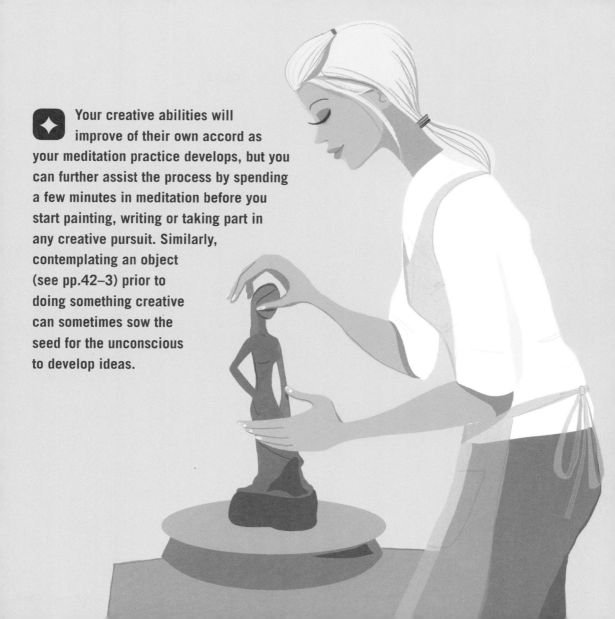

✦ Your creative abilities will improve of their own accord as your meditation practice develops, but you can further assist the process by spending a few minutes in meditation before you start painting, writing or taking part in any creative pursuit. Similarly, contemplating an object (see pp.42–3) prior to doing something creative can sometimes sow the seed for the unconscious to develop ideas.

Art as meditation

Painting and drawing are two of the most relaxing and rewarding of the arts. You can allow your unconscious to express itself spontaneously by keeping your mind clear and open when you are painting or drawing, just as you do in meditation. The Swiss psychotherapist Carl Jung discovered that his clients' paintings – often of mandalas (see pp.64–5) – showed remarkable development as their psychological health improved, and there is little doubt that when we draw and paint we express aspects of our inner experiences as meditators.

Sit at your desk or table, or stand at your easel and close your eyes. Watch your breath for a couple of moments to still your mind. Then, open your eyes, take up your brush or pencil and start working. Paint or draw from life if you wish, or from your imagination, memory or from abstract impressions.

Simply be mindful of the act of painting or drawing and allow it to take you where it will. Think of it as a meditation in itself, as well as a representation of your meditation practice. Display your art in your home and keep it as a record of your meditative journey. Allow it to teach you about yourself.

Play with poetry

Ultimate truth, the truth that lies beyond rational, materialistic science, is best expressed through symbols and metaphor, and nowhere do symbols and metaphor speak to us more directly than in poetry. This artform appeals to our feelings and our emotions as well as to our intellect. A line of poetry often tells us more than pages of prose, taking us to a reality that lies beyond the actual words, and that changes us in a way difficult to describe but impossible to forget.

Poems often provide good subjects for contemplation, and meditation also helps you to appreciate the true meaning of poetry, just as it assists you in appreciating the natural world and the gift of life. As with drawing and painting, meditation can also help you to create poetry yourself, because poetry arises best in a mind free from distractions and open to the unconscious. The best poetry is always initially spontaneous and inspirational, even if you polish it a little afterwards.

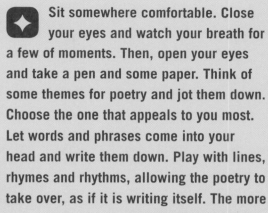

Sit somewhere comfortable. Close your eyes and watch your breath for a few of moments. Then, open your eyes and take a pen and some paper. Think of some themes for poetry and jot them down. Choose the one that appeals to you most. Let words and phrases come into your head and write them down. Play with lines, rhymes and rhythms, allowing the poetry to take over, as if it is writing itself. The more you do so, the more easily it will flow and the more it will reveal about yourself and the mysteries of existence.

Overcome setbacks

From time to time it is a good idea to review your meditation progress. A common problem that you might encounter is that after several days in which your ability to stay focused appears to be improving, you suddenly have a bad day when you can't keep your mind still. Why?

There are several reasons for this, but the two most likely are firstly, that your mind is too full of other things and you are finding it difficult to focus, and secondly that some of the novelty surrounding meditation has begun to wear off and you are losing your concentration along with your enthusiasm.

It is important not to be discouraged by such experiences or to abandon meditation as a bad job. As with any learning experience, setbacks are only to be expected. The secret is to persevere and work your way through them.

◆ One way to still a particularly active mind is to count each breath. Some teachers recommend this from the beginning, but I advise reserving it for when things are not going so well. Sit on your cushion on the floor or on a chair. Close your eyes and focus on your breath. Count on each out-breath from one up to 12, then start again at one. If you lose track of counting, just go back to one again. If your mind is still busy, try counting up to 12 and then backwards from 12 to one. This usually does the trick.

Following a path

Meditation is typically associated with one or other of the major psycho-spiritual paths, in particular those originating in the East, such as Hinduism, Jainism, Buddhism or Taoism. And faiths such as Christianity, Islam and Judaism also have long-established meditative traditions, although these generally attract less attention and are not always strongly emphasized as an essential element of spiritual development.

You may sometimes hear people say that you cannot make genuine progress in meditation unless you decide to follow one of these paths. It's true that it's sometimes difficult to find a good teacher unless you do so. However, nobody has a monopoly on meditation. Agnostics can meditate along with those who have spiritual beliefs. In fact, *anyone* can meditate because meditation is a natural quality of the mind, a quality with which we are born and which remains with us throughout life, whether we choose to make use of it or not.

So should you follow a path? The great psycho-spiritual traditions and faiths have many centuries of accumulated experience to call upon, and teachers from these traditions and faiths are able to give guidance and encouragement that is hard to find elsewhere. But even if you do not belong to their tradition or faith and have no wish to become a member, good teachers will not turn you away. Neither will they put pressure upon you to "convert" to their beliefs. But ultimately, only you can decide which, if any, path is the right one for you to follow.

Of course, if you are one of the many people who uses meditation simply as an effective means of relaxation and stress-reduction, you can continue to use it in this way. But if you wish, you can also allow the practice to take your mind to more profound levels. For many people this leads to a development in spiritual awareness and to the realization that they are much more than just their physical being. So, while meditation may not prompt you to follow any one tradition in particular, it will encourage you to decide for yourself what this realization means for you.

Working with a teacher

It is said that when the pupil is ready the teacher appears. I wish it was that simple! Usually, you have to go out and find one. You can learn meditation techniques from books such as this, and practise very well, but at some point it is helpful to have a teacher with whom to work. A good teacher can assess your progress, discuss any difficulties you are having and introduce you to additional techniques. They can also help to motivate you, and if they have a group of other students, you may find meditating in a group of like-minded people provides extra support (see pp.26–7).

How do you know if your teacher is good? In short, a good teacher will never extort money from you, attempt to push you too far too soon, introduce you to unsuitable techniques, attempt to distance you from your friends or family, or insist you follow their religion. If your teacher does any of these things, or you feel uncomfortable with any aspect of the guidance they offer, find someone else.

It can be particularly useful to discuss meditation difficulties with a teacher. Common problems are poor motivation, apparent lack of progress, physical pains caused by sitting, time constraints and troubling or confusing experiences while meditating. Such experiences include having visions – occasionally unpleasant ones but more frequently pleasant ones. Your teacher will advise you to ignore them, just as with thoughts. Another experience you might find troubling is an apparent increase in psychic abilities, such as telepathy. Although many scientists still dispute the existence of such abilities, carefully controlled experiments indicate beyond reasonable doubt that they are a reality. So why do they arise in meditation? It seems that when the mind is quiet, the subtle psychic impressions usually drowned out by mental activity can emerge into awareness. If you do have psychic experiences, try not to take them too seriously. A good teacher will be able to reassure you and encourage you to work through them, so that they do not divert you from the true purposes of meditation – finding calm, and growing personally and spiritually.

Conclusion

Meditation is the true experience of your own mind, uncluttered by the trivial things that clamour for attention and restrict you to living on the surface of your own being. Through meditation practice, you can learn far more about your true self than from writing a journal or from the comments of your friends' and family. Indeed, once you have enjoyed a brief taste of meditation, you will keep the experience with you always, and even if you stop for some reason, you are likely to be drawn back to it at some time in the future – as the saying goes: "Once a meditator, always a meditator".

Remember that meditation is a journey. And as with any journey, you have to remain patient along the way. It is particularly important not to give up at the first sign of difficulty. The main reason why people stop meditating, even if only temporarily, is that they become discouraged. Initially their progress seems good, then either it comes to a halt or goes into reverse. Why? Often it is because they stop making an effort, imagining that things will just happen by themselves. Even experienced meditators have to be wary of slipping into complacency, and allowing mental chatter or daydreaming to take over again. If you find yourself feeling discouraged, the best thing to do is simply to work through the confusion. Remind yourself that meditation is for everyone and that all of us, including you, can meditate. Provided you gently return your mind to your breath each time it wanders away, you will make progress – and it's on the bad days that you will make the most headway,

It is equally important to stay grounded and not get carried away with your practice when things appear to be going well. At such times you might find yourself becoming rather unworldly and detached from everyday life, with your attention firmly on the spiritual realms. If this happens, consciously return your focus to your everyday life and practise mindfulness, so that your mind is more present in the moment. It is this ordinary life that is realized as an expression of the ultimate reality from which everything arises and to which everything returns.

Further reading

If you would like to learn more about meditation, there are a number of useful books available to help you. Many of them are written from the viewpoint of a particular spiritual tradition – for example, Buddhist or Hindu – but others are more general. In any case, the fundamental techniques of meditation remain the same, no matter what the particular perspective of the writer or teacher concerned.

Listed opposite are a few personal recommendations of books that are not too technical and that provide good overviews of the subject in a friendly and accessible way. Reading more about meditation will not also help you to maintain your interest in the subject, but also remind you of the value of regular practice.

BOOKS

Fontana, David *Learn to Meditate*
(Duncan Baird Publishers, London, 1999)

Fontana, David *Learn Zen Meditation*
(Duncan Baird Publishers, London, 2001
and as *Discover Zen* Chronicle Books,
San Francisco, 2001)

Fontana, David *Meditation Week by Week*
(Duncan Baird Publishers, London, 2004)

Fontana, David *The Meditator's Handbook*
(Thorsons/Harper Collins, London, 2002)

Goleman, Daniel *The Meditative Mind*
(Aquarian Press, Wellingsborough, 1995
and Tarcher, Los Angeles, 1996)

LeShan, Lawrence *How to Meditate*
(Turnstone, London, 1983 and Brown & Co.,
New York, 1999)

McDonald, Kathleen *How to Meditate*
(Wisdom Publications, Boston, 1984)

Sharples, Bob *Meditation and Relaxation
in Plain English* (Wisdom Publications,
Boston, 2006)

Solé-Leris, Amadeo *Tranquillity and Insight*
(Pariyatti, Onalaska, WA, 1992)

Wallace, B. Alan *The Attention Revolution*
(Wisdom Publications, Boston,
2006)

Index